D0388163

In-Love and Loving It – Or Not!

A Users Guide to Love and Being In-Love

Richard Skerritt

In-Love and Loving It – Or Not!

A Users Guide to Love and Being In-Love

Richard Skerritt

Dalkeith Press
Kennett Square, Pennsylvania

Published in 2007 by
Dalkeith Press
873 East Baltimore Pike #742
Kennett Square, PA 19348 USA

Library of Congress Control Number: not yet
assigned

Softcover Edition
ISBN: 978-1-933369-05-1

Also available in PDF e-book Edition:
ISBN: 978-1-933369-06-X

Cover Image used under license from Corbis.

Second Printing - January 2009

Notice

This book documents the personal experience and perspectives of the author.

While the author has quite a lot of experience and insight into relationships, he is not a psychologist, psychiatrist, counselor, or therapist. This book may contribute to your understanding of your situation. Still, it is not a substitute for professional help.

Falling in love can sometimes be a very painful experience. If you are in distress, please seek help from someone trained to help you. Your personal or family doctor is often a good person to seek help from. They can rule out any physical problems, prescribe mediation if needed, and suggest a counselor or therapist if appropriate.

Contents

Introduction

Old black and white movies; *Beauty and the Beast*; happily ever after: man, we all want to fall in love. It's the way the universe tells us who we belong with forever and ever. Nothing could be better. And sometimes, it works out that way... and sometimes **not**.

So you're in love, or you want to fall in love, or you want to get out of love, or you want her to fall in love with you. The problem is that it just doesn't seem to work like it does in the movies. **Damn!**

The truth is that love is complicated. Under the best of circumstances, falling-in-love can be joyful and exhilarating; under the worst it can be brutally painful.

This little book will try to help you understand how it all works and make it work better for you.

Conscious/Unconscious

I'm not going to hold you up long before I get into the good stuff, but if you're going to understand what falling-in-love is all about, you're going to have to get comfortable with the idea that our minds work on more than one level. We all recognize the *conscious* part of our minds which includes all the thoughts and emotions that we are aware of.

There is another level on which our minds function; a level about which we are only indirectly aware. This is the unconscious (sometimes called subconscious). We probably all know that this part of our mind performs some basic regulation of our breathing and heartbeat. But there are much more sophisticated things going on in our unconscious.

Our unconscious mind is really the home to our life energy – our spirit – and seems to serve primarily to protect that spirit and what it calls us to be. It can do this by helping us get away from things. For example, we react to a loud noise before we consciously can think about what it is.

Our unconscious mind can also help us to get things that we need. Sometimes it may do this in a somewhat subversive way, overriding our conscious decisions. Freudian slips, where we unintentionally use a word with a very different meaning than we consciously intended, are an example of such direct unconscious control.

But most of the time our unconscious influences us through feelings. Rather than taking control directly as if we were robots, our unconscious simply sends us a strong motivation in the form of feeling or emotion.

The most common, and unfortunate, emotion that arises from our unconscious is a feeling of depression. When we're in situations that are hurtful to us, our unconscious responds by generating feelings of sadness, despair, or anger, all of which could (and hopefully will) motivate us to make changes in our situation.

But enough about that. What you're really interested in is falling in love. And falling-in-love is another very powerful emotion set upon us from within by our unconscious. It is purposeful and intended to motivate us to seek something that we need to be healthy. And that brings us to…

Section 1 - Falling in Love

Falling in Love - How it Happens

Briefly, *falling in love* is an unconsciously motivated state, not too far removed from mental illness, in which we attempt to meet our needs by completing ourselves in sexual union with another person and emotional dependence on that person. Falling in love is a state of powerful feeling which motivates thoughts and actions. In contrast, as we'll see later, *loving* is a chosen, purposeful effort, often done in the face of fear, to nurture our own growth as a person, or the growth of another.

Wow. Are you still with me? I know this seems pretty radical, but there is a lot here you can use to get in control of your life. Trust me.

In Rapture? Or Insane?

Falling In Love: Old black and white movies; *Beauty and the Beast*; happily ever after. Man, we all want to fall in love. It's the way the universe tells us who we belong with forever and ever. And nothing could be better. Except...

Falling in love is a lot like mental illness in disguise. Mental illness?!! Yes, that's what I said. Falling in love is a lot like mental illness in disguise. Here's a short catalog of what's wrong with falling in love:

- First, love overcomes us with excitement, fulfillment, and euphoria. Fun – yes. But rational or reasonable? No. It's possible to fall in love with someone who we might not even know. Doesn't sound very healthy to me.
- Second, we lose all perspective about the person we're in love with. We idealize the person. They become the most beautiful/handsome, most loving, caring, kindest... Really?
- Third, being in love doesn't last. The fairy tales say it will. And

sometimes we might know a couple that we say is still "in love" after 40 or 50 years. But it's not so. Eventually reality sinks in and the glow is lost. Being in love is just a transient state of altered emotions and awareness. That 40+ year couple isn't in love, they've transitioned to loving, which is totally different. The problem with this is that we can be motivated to make decisions with lifelong impact based on an emotional state that doesn't last nearly that long.

- Fourth, we lose ourselves in emotional dependence. Without our understanding it, our whole ego – our sense of who we are – tries to merge with our love. We become incomplete without them. We need that person to be whole. It's a nice romantic concept. But it's not very healthy. Have you ever been in love with someone who didn't love you back? I have. And it isn't any fun at all. Trust me.

- Fifth, we can't control it. We don't choose to fall in love, and we don't choose who we fall in love with. Later I'll talk more about the factors that influence who we might fall in love with. But the bottom line is that it isn't a conscious choice.

- Sixth, falling in love always happens with someone that's a possible sexual partner. It just won't happen outside of that, because it is driven by our inherent need to make strong babies. This could be ok, but sometimes the underlying drive to fall in love isn't sexual, but rather about needs that arise from our incompleteness as a person. And the choices for who can fulfill those needs are greatly limited if only potential sexual partners are in the running.

So, when you're in love:

- You get there without choice;
- You didn't get to choose who you're in love with;
- The one you're in love with has to be from the limited set of people you can be sexually attracted to;

- You can't think straight, because everything is idealized;
- You can't feel straight, because you're lost in euphoria (or dysphoria if she doesn't love you back); and
- You can't be whole by yourself.

As nice as euphoria may feel, you can do a lot of damage to yourself when you're lost in this fog. Or, you may find the love of your life.

Which is it? How can you tell?

The Perfect Story?

Everything I'm about to say is my understanding, which I've assembled from a lot of reading, careful thought, observation, and my own experiences – both joyful and painful. These ideas can't be proven right nor can they be proven wrong. They can, however, help you to understand why you have the feelings you do and what it will take to satisfy the needs that motivated those feelings.

What it's about

What falling-in-love is all about is getting a man and woman together and keeping them together, so that they can create and raise strong babies and so they can emotionally nurture one another.

Where it Came From

The emotional forces that today we call falling-in-love were developed over thousands of years when humans lived in small hunter-gatherer clans. In this society, men were hunters who spent their days away from the clan hunting. Women and children stayed in the clan. Disease, injury, and malnutrition continually challenged these people. The strongest survived; the weaker did not.

Any patterns of behavior that led to a man-woman pairings that produced healthy babies who grew up to be survivors were selected and passed down to succeeding generations. Patterns that produced less strong babies or less hardy children/adults had less chance of being passed on; they were deselected.

Over tens of thousands of years, humans developed innate patterns of responses and behavior that increased the chances of making babies that survived. These patterns are genetic, and we all inherit them today.

Although we would all like to think we control our lives and make our own decisions in conscious choice, when it comes to falling in love, it simply isn't that way. The responses that we inherit from these primitive times do not originate with thought. They originate in unconscious processing, in a **pattern recognition** process, a process that then seeks to control our actions by motivating us with powerful emotions.

Thus, a key to understanding how and why we fall in love is to know the patterns that our minds unconsciously recognize and respond to.

His Job

In early clans, survival was difficult. A woman who was pregnant or had small children was busy and limited in what she could do for herself. She had to rely on her partner to provide for her. So her success as a parent depended on choosing a **strong provider**. In those times, this meant a **strong hunter**.

The best hunters had characteristics – mostly behaviors – that set them apart. These are important because over time women have evolved to be responsive to this pattern of male behavior.

A good hunter can be recognized by these traits:

- A good hunter is **confident**. He's been doing his thing for a long time and he has no doubt about his ability. Fear is not part of his makeup.
- A good hunter is **focused**. He is busy with his job. He is not hanging around passing time.
- A good hunter is **aware** of his surroundings. He has to be, to spot prey, but he also picks up and recognizes the presence of people around him, including available women. But he is focused on his task, so he doesn't dwell on other people.
- A good hunter travels **alone**. While most hunters liked to stay in groups for safety, the strongest would venture out on their own.
- A good hunter is **strong**. He has to be able to overcome his prey, and his strength shows in the way he moves and the way he looks.

- A good hunter is **consistent** over time. He doesn't drift away or take time off. He stays at his task day after day, month after month.

Today still, women carry the innate programming to respond to this pattern in men. In a little bit we'll see how this comes together in how we fall in love.

Notice that most of these traits are behaviors. There are some that depend on physical appearance, but mostly the key traits are behavioral. We see this reflected in today's standards of attractiveness for men, which don't rely strongly on appearance.

Her Job

The demands on a woman in this early setting were different. Since she stayed in the safety of the clan, she didn't need hunter characteristics. To make strong, viable children, she needed to able to **conceive** children and **stay healthy** herself to deliver and care for them. Thus, her success as a parent depended on her being a **fertile, healthy individual**.

Today we see in our society that there is tremendous focus on the appearance of women, while men seem to escape this scrutiny. This comes from this early need for men to choose fertile, healthy women to partner with. To find them, they looked for certain physical characteristics that we can all recognize in today's idea of beauty.

A fertile, healthy woman can be recognized by these traits:

- She is **young**. Fertility ends later in life, and in these difficult times, conception may also have been difficult.
- She is **sexually healthy** and fully mature. This can be recognized in physical characteristics:
  - A narrow waist;
  - Broad hips;
  - Full breasts.
- She is **physically healthy**. This can be recognized by:
  - Bright, clear eyes;
  - Shiny, full hair;
  - Clear skin.
- She **does not have children** already. The key marker for this is a **flat, trim abdomen**.

Today still, men carry the innate programming to respond to this pattern in women, and women strive to fit the pattern. This isn't just social insanity! It's our inborn selection system at work. Again, we'll see how this comes together in how we fall in love.

What's needed in her

So far we have set the stage for falling in love by defining the natural patterns that men and women are programmed to respond to. But, we don't want everybody getting all excited about everybody else all the time. That would be chaotic.

What we see is that the pattern matching responses are switched on by certain circumstances. In women, there are two things needed to switch this search system on:

- First, she must be fully sexually mature and ready to conceive. Today, this seems to happen around age 16.
- Second, she must be unattached. Having a regular relationship with a man will inhibit these search reactions. So she must be physically and emotionally unattached.

When both of these criteria are met, a woman's innate pattern matching responses are switched on, and she will find herself responding to men who have "strong hunter" characteristics.

What's needed in him

Men seem to also have some natural programming for when their pattern systems are activated. For men, it appears that they also need to be ready for this ideal partnering process.

In men, the pattern matching responses are triggered or switched on by these two things:

- He must be an established, proven provider. We know from psychologists that we spend the first part of our adult lives working to demonstrate mastery of our world, and then transition to a focus more on internal needs. It seems that this mastery is important in switching on the pattern responses in men. Have you ever wondered why younger men seem disinterested in having children, even though they may be married to a woman who is anxious to have children? Younger men haven't established this standing as proven providers.
- Like women, he must be unattached. Having a consistent physical and emotional partner seems to suppress these partnering responses.

Beauty chooses

The old saying is that "beauty chooses," and so it seems to work in this process. It is **not**, however, a choice made with thought and reason. It happens in the unconscious part of our minds and may surprise us with feelings that are very strong.

The "choice" that happens here is the pattern match. When a woman who is ready is around a man with the right pattern of "strong hunter" traits, her pattern recognition will "click" onto him. We're not talking about finding someone that mom will approve of. We're not talking about a thoughtful choice. We're talking about an innate selection process operating at a subconscious level.

Most of the pattern elements can be observed fairly quickly. But there is one that takes time: **consistency**. Remember that the age-old selection process is looking for a man who will stick with her through child-raising. So a single exposure to a man won't do it. She needs to see him repeatedly so that he shows that not only does he have the right stuff, but he's consistent. A little later I'll say some about the individual traits that we are biased toward, but these don't change the basic process.

So, when a woman who is ready is repeatedly around a man who consistently shows the right traits, she'll suddenly find that she has "clicked" onto him.

Once she clicks, her feelings and behavior will change. She'll now find herself working to get his attention. Remember, he's a hunter, busy with his task. So she'll have to get in front of him. She'll have to make herself part of his surroundings. So she'll consistently position herself to be where he'll see her.

And she'll need to let him know that she has the "right stuff." Her behavior becomes open, and much more submissive. Not only does she have the right appearance, but she now behaves differently than the other women around him. A bright smile with bright eyes will become automatic when she looks at him. And she'll feel especially aware of her appearance, even though she may not consciously choose to, taking special care to look good: hair, skin, and figure all showing that she has it.

Strength is subverted

Now the stage has been set, and assuming the man is ready, his pattern matching systems will kick in for him, as well. Again, it has nothing to do with logic or reason, but is a process happening in the unconscious part of the mind that gives rise to powerful feelings.

In this situation, as she presents herself to him in a submissive way, and repeatedly shows the right physical traits, he will respond by being attracted to her. His focus on work/task will be broken, and he'll find himself drawn to her.

Irresistible force

And this, my friends, is what we call falling in love. She focused on him; he focused on her, and both feeling strong feelings of attraction.

At this point, the emotional forces become almost irresistible. Physical touch between the two will accelerate and amplify the attraction. His touch will trigger her to submit to him, and she'll find herself melting in his arms.

Sexual attraction becomes almost overpowering. Remember, the whole idea was to make a strong baby! How will that happen? Sex! Both the man and the woman will feel a tremendous drive and excitement. What happens then is matter of choice and self-control, but there is no doubt about the motivation that both will feel.

All radar down

Now, assuming there is nothing preventing the attraction from unfolding, both the man and woman are in an emotional and physical relationship. With the continual sensory input, neither now meets that necessary condition – being unattached – that's necessary for this partnering process to work. Thus, both have their natural radar switch off, preventing their reaction to other men and women around them. They are now together and stabilized as partners.

This is the essence of falling in love, in its most ideal form. Later I'll say more about how this could happen in a less than ideal way.

Why Am I In Love?

In giving us motivation – through feelings – to fall in love, nature is trying to satisfy some very basic needs for us. If we understand these needs, we can help to make ourselves less vulnerable to falling-in-love with the wrong person or in a bad situation, and thus more able to fall in love with the right person in a good situation.

There are two underlying needs driving us to fall in love: mating and emotional nurturing. When we fall in love, our unconscious is trying to satisfy these inherent needs: to have a partner and produce children; and to receive emotional support and nurturing in our life.

Mating

I described mating needs already in the section on how it works. Producing viable, successful children was what set our ancestors apart from their contemporaries whose children didn't live to pass on their genes. So we still carry these strong genetic programs that lead us to seek a successful mate and produce children.

What strengthens this drive? Simple! Part of the drive to fall in love is to help us find mating partners. This part of the drive will be stronger when we're without a mate, and is reduced when we're in a situation that feels like we've found a mate. If we have a stable relationship that provides physical contact and sex, we're much less likely to fall in love with someone other than our current partner. If we don't have someone to touch and have sex with, then our unconscious mind is much more likely to guide us to zero in on someone and "fall us" into love with that person.

Emotional Nurturing

The other part of the drive to fall in love – emotional nurturing – is more complicated. I think there are really two parts to this. First, there is a natural need for love, affection, and nurture. All healthy adults need this to some extent. For most of us, this is something we need daily or nearly so.

24

The second part has to do with feeling complete. We all have many dimensions to our personality and our interests and motivations in life. To feel complete, we need to somehow satisfy all those diverse interests. And most of us don't do this. There are areas we have developed in our lives, but there are other interests or motivations that we've ignored. We can make it feel like we've fulfilled these undeveloped areas – at least in part – by close association with someone else.

The best explanation I have found for this is by Harville Hendrix in his book *Getting the Love You Want*. Hendrix believes we have two ways we force ourselves to be incomplete. The first is *denying* parts of ourselves, and the second is *hiding* parts of ourselves. Both are ways that we refuse to express aspects of our life energy or spirit. The first arises because we cannot accept that we have those traits, and the second because we choose to avoid others' reactions to those traits by not showing them.

According to Hendrix:

- We deny parts of ourselves because family and society disapprove. I might be a big hulking guy and love floral wallpaper. Not for long, I guess. It would be too painful. Better to just deny that part of me and go with plain off-white.

- We lose parts of ourselves because we fail to recognize them or don't nurture them. For example, I might have been an athlete in high school, but in my years studying quantum mechanics and later working hard at the laboratory bench trying to count all those quanta, I could adopt a sedentary lifestyle and lose the physical aspect of myself.

These denied and incomplete parts are more than just empty spaces. They are unmet needs. As people, we are not complete without them. They are deficiencies that are felt by our spirit. Our spirit always wants us to become all of what we should be. By associating closely with someone, we can provide to our spirit some of those undeveloped aspects without us having to develop them. In place of growing ourselves into all the dimensions we could grow into, we sub in our partner.

How Can I Get Better control?

We all know that being in love can be a powerful experience. The problem comes when everything isn't just right. Then we wish that it might be more consciously controlled, so we could step away from a painful situation. Unfortunately, it's not something we can simply control, but there are things we can do get some control. We can get better control by doing things that reduce the unconscious drives to fall in love.

Grab a partner - The first thing we can do to reduce the drive to fall in love is to put ourselves into something that feels to our unconscious like a mating relationship. A steady relationship in which we are touched, hugged, cuddled can go a long way. If you are ready for it, and the situation allows, a regular sexual relationship will probably satisfy this unconscious need completely.

The flip side of this is something to be aware of, also. If you solidify this physical relationship, you may take the impetus out of the drive to find someone else. Thus, you can run the risk of idling in a relationship that isn't what you want, and not finding the person who could be what you want. So it's something to use with some caution.

Nurture yourself - the second thing we can do to reduce the drive to fall in love is to provide for our own emotional nurturing. Let's take the two parts of this separately.

The first way for us to provide our own emotional nurturing it is through day-to-day emotional support. An example of this might be moving back in with mom. Seriously? Well, yes, at least in principle. Establishing new friendships or working to strengthen the contact in existing family or friendly relationships is another way to do this. The key thing here is that this kind of day-to-day emotional support comes from someone else who cares about us. And we have to be in contact from day to day to get the support.

If you think about this, it pretty much fits with the pattern that many young adults follow in their lives. Young adults frequently have a group of close friends that they rely upon day to day for emotional support and encouragement. But once we move out of the highly structured worlds of high school and college, these kinds of friendship situations become more difficult to establish. Nevertheless, they are a model we can work toward to establish greater emotional independence in any life situation.

The second part of nurturing ourselves emotionally is the harder part. This is working to make ourselves more complete as people. To do this, we have to figure out what a complete 'me' would be.

To make ourselves complete, we have to first to discover these unrealized aspects of ourselves. This may be easy or not. It really depends on how self-aware we are and also on how many opportunities we have had to chase our desires and dreams. There may be one big thing looming, like "I've always wanted to write a book," or there may be many small things. Figuring this out will take some quiet time, some reflection, thinking back on the joys in our past.

Usually, we know of some lost loves, things that we used to do that we put aside for one reason or another. We also have hopes and dreams, things we may have thought of doing or wished that we could do, yet never tried to do or didn't try hard enough to do. These might be good starting points for personal growth.

And once we have an idea of what we need to do to make ourselves more complete, we then face the hard work of pushing outside of our comfort zone and really trying to make those new things happen. We might be able to make a significant change quickly. For example, if my dream was to learn to ride horses, simply buying some clothes and equipment and then starting to take lessons might be enough to give me a much better feeling about myself. On the other hand, if my dream was to write a book, it might take years to bring that to full realization.

The more we can discover and develop ourselves as complete individuals, the greater the emotional foundation we build for ourselves, and the more emotional stability we have. And this emotional stability reduces the need - felt at an unconscious level - which drives us to fall in love. As more complete people, we have less need to replace the undeveloped parts of ourselves, and thus we are less vulnerable to developing strong feelings of being in love as a way of filling that need.

Who is the lucky one?

Our Ideal – Imago

We all realize that we are more attracted to some people than to others. Sometimes these tendencies are good, and sometimes they're not so good, but we all have some. I struggled to understand why I was drawn toward certain types of women. Things started to come clear for me when I read about the idea of imago in Harville Hendrix's book *Getting the Love You Want.*

Hendrix believes we each have a fairly permanent image, which he calls the imago, based on the characteristics of our primary caregivers as young children. This image is maintained in our subconscious mind, where we're not really aware of it, and it includes the shortcomings of those early life caregivers, including how we were hurt or neglected by them.

According to Hendrix's theory, this image determines who we will fall in love with. When we meet an imago match, we quickly feel like we've always known him, we can't remember being without him. We feel that we aren't complete without him, that we must have him. Our subconscious is overjoyed at finding the person who once had cared for us, and will now resume and make everything right. Romantic love overwhelms us and makes us behave in unselfish ways, and see only the good in the person.

I like parts of Hendrix's model. There definitely are certain characteristics that we are prone to feel attracted to, and others we are not so prone to. We can often see the pattern by looking at the series of chosen relationships we've had. But my own experience suggests that the characteristics we're attracted to are learned, and can be relearned. For example, I had always been attracted to very slender women. Then I had a relationship, one that started very much like I described in the previous section, and the woman had a lot more curve in her shape. My preferences changed! Now I find I'm attracted to both characteristics.

Who Is the Lucky One?

Whether there is a fixed imago or not, what's important to recognize here is that, at any moment, there are certain characteristics, unique to each of us, that we are attracted to. It probably isn't really important where the traits come from. What is important is becoming aware of what those traits are. Some of them may be of no particular significance to the success of our relationships. For example, I tend to be inherently drawn to women with dark hair. Since there are plenty of women with dark hair and since it doesn't seem to present any particular difficulties, this is just something I need to be aware of. For this kind of inherent preference, I need to keep in mind that if I become involved with someone who doesn't have that characteristic, there is somewhat less likelihood that I will fall in love with her.

However, there are traits that we may have natural preferences for that can hurt us. In my case, there was a period where I was naturally drawn to women who presented themselves in a way that I would now characterize as being depressed. I think this came about because my experience was that such women were easier to get close to than healthier women. Unfortunately, the women with this characteristic that I did become close to ended up having serious

In Love and Loving It – Or Not!

problems, depression included – which led to my relationship problems. So recognizing this preference was an important realization for me.

And I found that I was able to teach myself different preferences. I had been quite seriously hurt emotionally by the women I was involved with. And so I started watching to detect when I found myself attracted to a woman who seemed depressed. While there was really nothing I could do in any particular instance to stop that feeling of attraction, the initial feeling that I had was a mild one and something that I could simply turn my attention away from. And so, rather than following that mild feeling of attraction, I took it as a warning signal and deliberately turned my attention away from such people. Instead, I deliberately focus my attention toward women with opposite characteristics: bright eyes and ready smiles. With time I found that I no longer have that automatic attraction, and I am more naturally drawn to a woman who presents a happier image.

Who's there?

The other thing about who we fall in love with is almost too obvious. Have you ever heard of someone that fell in love with another person that they never knew?

34

Who Is the Lucky One?

Obviously, we only fall in love with people that we are somehow exposed to. And primarily, these are people we are around with some regularity.

So? If you read the section on how things work, then you may have a better idea who around you might be someone that your unconscious will pick out for you to fall in love with. Don't want to fall in love with that person? Maybe we should think about not being around that person as much. Because the reality here is that if you are unattached and emotionally healthy and you are around someone who has the right characteristics, there is a finite possibility that you will fall in love with that person. This applies more strongly to women, because the characteristics in man that draw a woman to fall in love are not dependent on the man paying special attention to the woman. Thus a woman is more likely to fall in love with a man who has no special interest in the woman. Men are not immune to this risk. But if you remember the way things work, a woman's open behavior toward a man is important in getting him to fall in love with her.

And what if you find yourself in love with someone, and want that person to reciprocate the feeling? Well, you better make sure that you get yourself around that person on a regular basis. Because it is highly unlikely that he or she will fall in love with you if you are not around.

When it Goes Awry

Well, a perfect story. Man and woman find one another by falling in love. Don't we all wish?

The problem is that it doesn't always work that way. Remember, these processes are unconscious, and they're pattern matching. We don't have a committee of learned experts checking every trait to make sure it's valid. No one is reviewing the data to make sure the behavior is sincere. And what if the pattern is *almost* compete, but not complete?

The sad reality is that our partnering reactions can be triggered at the wrong time and with the wrong person. And when that happens, we find ourselves in love with someone who doesn't love us back, or worse yet, someone who's bad for us. That, I can tell you from personal experience, is **no** fun.

How can it happen? Well, look at the pattern that women respond to. There isn't anything in that pattern that selects for men who are available. A man in a long-term, stable partnership, and so isn't vulnerable to his partnering reactions, may still exhibit all the necessary traits to triggers a woman's attraction to him. Then she finds herself feeling in-love with him, yet he doesn't respond because he's not programmed to. And, socially, he's expected not to.

Or look at the pattern that men respond to. The first part of this pattern is all about how she looks. A woman can look in a way exhibits most of the traits that trigger a man's attraction, yet she may not be paying any special attention to him. Thus he may find himself drawn to a woman who has no interest at all in him. In fact he may not even have the right traits to attract someone like her, yet still find himself locked onto her.

The second part of the pattern that draws men is behavioral: submissiveness on the part of the woman. There are many situations in our society in which a woman

is required to be submissive. A woman
whose boss is a man is a great example.
Here, she's expected to allow her boss to
play a dominant role. And men's pattern
selection is fuzzy. She's not attracted to
him, and isn't trying to draw him to her; yet
staying within the job role may still trigger
his attraction to her.

Mental Illness and Falling in Love - And
then there is mental illness. Most people
don't associate mental illness with falling in
love. To most people, mental illness means
someone acting bizarre and crazy. But the
reality is that most mental illness is harder
to see in people. It is often covered with a
façade of normal behavior. Sometimes the
disease itself even causes an amplification
of positive traits – a deception.

Thus, ill people can appear to be wonderful,
amazing people… for a while – long
enough to trigger all our partnering
reactions and in-love feelings. Then, the
façade breaks and we find ourselves in-love
with someone who is totally incapable of
fulfilling their role in a stable emotional and
physical relationship. In the worst case, this
can happen after marriage, leaving the
healthy spouse trapped in a social situation
that forbids seeking emotional support
outside the marriage, yet married to

someone who is incapable of providing that support.

I'm in love with him. How do I get him?

OK, so that one special guy has captured you. You know that you fell in love with him, and you want him to fall in love with you. So what do you do?

Before we start messing around with you and what you do, remember that there are two qualities that he must have for you to successfully attract him. First of all, he must be physically and emotionally available. This means he's not in a relationship currently that's providing him with emotional or physical nurturing. And second, he has to be reasonably emotionally healthy.

Before you start spending a lot of time and energy trying to attract him, you should at least make an effort to figure out where he stands in these two dimensions. Being in an intimate relationship shuts down the pattern matching mechanism that you need to use to draw him to you. So it's pointless to pursue someone that is in a satisfying relationship already.

His emotional health may be hard for you to judge, but it should be a concern to you. There are many unhealthy people around us, and sometimes they can present themselves as a very capable and attractive people. But it's what's inside that counts, and if he has a significant metal health problem, he is not going to respond to you in the way a healthy person would. Even if he does so initially, the relationship will almost certainly sour later on, and that can be very hurtful.

There are two things to look for here. First, if he is totally perfect in every way, that's a warning sign that he's not genuine. The second is him doing things, no matter how small, that make you wonder, or make you feel a little funny. Most people with problems will do one or both of these things. You have to be sensitive, though, because the fact that you're already in love with him means you'll be inclined to dismiss these peculiarities as unimportant.

I'm in Love with Him – How Do I Get Him?

But often they signal an underlying problem that is being concealed.

So if he's not already involved with someone, he's not too perfect, and you can't pick up any warning signs of behavior that seems strange or unsettling to you, then you can start working on the things you can do to attract him to fall in love with you.

Remember, this is all about matching the pattern. You need to present yourself to him, repeatedly, showing him qualities that will trigger his response to you. You'll have to show him a combination of physical appearance and behavior to do that.

The behavior you need to show is submissive. You need to get yourself in front of him, make sustained eye contact, and smile. Now that shouldn't be too hard. After all, you're in love with him! Greet him and stay open for his response. You're trying to show him behavior that is different from most women, and to do this you'll allow him to control the length of time that you interact. If he wants to say hello and turn away, you smile and watch him go. If he wants to talk, talk. Let him be in control. You are presenting a pattern that shows you are submissive to him.

You also have to show him the physical characteristics that will trigger him to be drawn to you: small waist and full hips, full shiny hair, bright eyes and their skin. Don't be shy about showing what you've got. Styles now are really helpful since you can easily wear shirts that hug your waist and tight pants that show the shape of your hips.

Remember, it's a small waist broadening into wide hips that shows that you're fully mature as a woman, and while his conscious thoughts might be focused somewhere else, these are the features that trigger his subconscious pattern matching. Hair is important too, and if your hair is long you have an advantage. It's just that the more you have, the easier it is to show the fullness and shine. If your hair isn't the greatest, try working on it to get it closer to the ideal. Remember, it's not about what he thinks he likes, but about what his unconscious patterning will respond to.

You're going to have to be willing to stick with this for a while. Triggering his pattern requires you to be in front of him many times, especially if you're around him in a setting where he's already very focused on a task. Men are naturally task-focused, and when he is intently working on something, it will be difficult for you to break that focus and get into his awareness. When he's more relaxed and less busy, it'll be easier for you to make an impression on him. You may need to make eye contact and interact with him many times to trigger a pattern match.

Of course, there is no guarantee that it will happen. We each have certain physical characteristics we are most responsive to. For example I happen to be naturally attracted to women with very dark hair, dark eyes and olive complexion. I'm much less strongly attracted to fair-skinned, red headed women. Your characteristics may match his preferences, or not. If you do match, he's likely to be more open to you, and this will help. If not, your task will be harder, but don't give up. As long as you have most of the pattern traits, you have a chance.

I'm In Love with Her. Now What?

So, you fell in love with a woman and you want her to fall in love with you. What do you do?

Remember, there are two things necessary here that you don't control – in addition to presenting yourself to her as having the right characteristics of a strong hunter, Just as I described in the analogous situation for a woman seeking to coax a man into love with her, for men it's also important that a woman not be in an intimate relationship that provides physical or emotional nurturing, and she must be reasonably emotionally healthy.

And as I described already for women, you need to be tuned in and willing to recognize subtle indicators that something is wrong. People that are emotionally unhealthy sometimes present themselves in a way that seems too perfect - almost like a dream come true. They may also give you some telltale signs that things are not right. Again, these may be things that you would be inclined to overlook or dismiss as unimportant. But if your guts tell you something just doesn't feel right, there is a very good chance that things are not right.

If she's just too perfect or you picked up some troubling signs for her, then you may find that despite all your best efforts she won't be attracted to you. Even worse is the dream come true scenario: she's immediately and completely attracted to you and everything is unrealistically wonderful. But someone like this can reverse their feelings without warning, suddenly and totally rejecting you, and this kind of emotional whipsaw can be devastating to you.

If she's unattached and there are no warning signs, then the coast is clear for you to do your best to attract her. But the way you do this is by not doing. You won't attract her by pursuing. It's the opposite of what people think, because this isn't about thinking. Forget the flowers and fancy dinners. Forget the valentines. She's not programmed to respond to that kind of behavior. Even though she says she wants them, they are not things that are going to draw her to you.

What will draw her to you is for you to be around her where she can see you be busy being a man. And as described earlier, she'll be attracted to behavior like that of a strong hunter. He's task focused; he's strong; he travels alone; he's confident; and he is aware of people around him but not distracted by them. It really doesn't matter if you are or aren't naturally confident. It's the behavior that she'll respond to. Faking it *is* the same as making it.

You need to be around her without being there for the obvious purpose of being around her. In other words, you need to have something that you're doing. If you don't have a way to be around here where you're preoccupied with your work, then present yourself that way anyway. This means you won't linger anyplace, including around her. When you speak with her it should be for a purpose. If not, then it should be perfunctory; somewhat of a, "Oh, I didn't see you there." And then go on about your business. Don't hang with the guys when you're around her.

This approach isn't what is obvious or expected. Remember, you need her to choose you. If you're choosing her first, and acting that way, you're not giving her the right signals that can match her pattern and encourage her to fall for you.

And, just as for women, there will be natural preferences that will be working for or against you in features like hair color and complexion. At this point, there is not much you can do about these, and probably you won't even know what those preferences are, or whether they favor you or disadvantage you. All you can do is keep in mind that, as much as you want it, it may not be the most natural thing for her to be drawn to you. Just do the best you can to present the right stuff.

I'm In Love - How Do I Get Out?

OK, you fell in love. And for whatever reason, the person you're in love with didn't reciprocate, or broke off the relationship. There isn't any hope of fixing things, so what do you do?

Let's try to get at what is happening. Remember that "falling in love" is essentially an insane state. It is nature's way to hook us into a permanent relationship.

The problem is that insanity is insane. Being in love compromises our ability to control our own lives. Our ego boundaries are compromised, and we don't feel whole in and of ourselves. And our reasoning about our lover is short circuited with blatant idealizations.

To answer "what do I do while I'm in love?" you need to look a little deeper. Remember that falling in love is a vehicle to get our needs met - our need for a mating relationship and our need for emotional nurturing. It's a means to get physical nurturing, and to fill in the incomplete parts of ourselves.

So if you want to get unstuck from being in love with someone who doesn't love you back, then you are going to have to find a way to meet your needs without him or her.

Chances are, no matter what you do, the intense emotions will not pass quickly. However, there are some things you can do that will expedite the process. Remember I talked about these back in the section about what drives the falling-in-love process?

First of all, you can develop nurturing relationships that can give you some of the day-to-day emotional support you need. Family and close friends can provide this, and you need to establish daily contact to get it.

Second, you can start working on developing those unrealized parts of yourself. As you develop these puzzle pieces and put them into place, your unconscious mind won't need to go out fishing for them in your lover. You'll become happier and more complete in and of yourself, and you'll reduce the in-love drive to meet these needs through another.

Then, you need to take advantage of the mechanism your unconscious used to get you in love in the first place. Your unconscious was essentially shopping for someone to fall in love with. Remember the image - the pattern for who you will fall in love with? That's the shopping list. Well, your unconscious has picked out model A. And that's who you're in love with.

But keep in mind that the unconscious is working with a fairly vague pattern, having blurred, general features. There are thousands of people who are "close enough" to match our patterns. So if we can do some conscious shopping, our unconscious is going to be coming along on those trips. And it's very possible, especially if we're not seeing the object of our in-love feelings any more, that our unconscious might decide that model B looks pretty good, too.

So, while it may feel totally empty and false to you, by exposing yourself to others, you enable your unconscious mechanisms to work - the same mechanisms that got you in love with the person you're in love with now. That mechanism might just up and change your feelings around to point toward somebody else. And if you're reading this, chances are that somebody couldn't be much worse than what you've got, and they might be a darned sight better.

But you have to be around other people for that to work. So getting around other people is critical to moving on. Your unconscious isn't too swift, and especially if it's already hooked on someone, it might take a lot of exposure to capture its attention. But being around people is good for us anyway, so this remedy can't possibly hurt, even if it's not entirely successful.

Last comes the mating relationship. Falling in love drives us toward potential mating partners. Our sexual drive is an essential piece of what makes this go. So falling in love is, in part, a way to get sex.

Well, if you don't like the way you're being driven to get sex by your unconscious, you might try getting some with your conscious. Again, by proactively meeting your own needs, you reduce the drive toward falling you into love that your unconscious has. And this fits in just great with the last remedy of being around people. If you're going to be around people, you might as well enjoy it. This option might not work for everyone, but it's something to keep in mind. Abstinence from sex has its virtue, but we are inherently sexual beings, and we need to keep in mind that we're trying to stand fast against a current when we do this.

It won't be fast, and not likely easy, either. But building nurturing relationships; working on your undeveloped self; exposing yourself to many others; and meeting your sexual needs by chosen relationships can all help to extricate you from the clutches of your unconscious when it has fallen you into love with someone who is bad for you, or just plain won't love you back.

Section 2 - Love

Loving – a Whole Different Matter

Well, we've talked about being in-love – a euphoric and sometimes unhealthy state used by our unconscious to get us into mating relationships and to meet our needs for nurturing.

But there's another concept here – one that often goes by the same name, yet has an entirely different foundation. That concept is love.

Love: I think that a great way to look at love is the way defined by M Scott Peck in his classic book *The Road Less Traveled.* He tells us that love is work, usually courageous, expended to nurture the spiritual growth of myself or another. It is a choice. And it is work. No idealism here.

No euphoria. No loss of ourselves. And no agony if it isn't returned.

What is spiritual growth? It is the growth of ourselves as human beings - as complete human beings. Remember Hendrix's lost or denied aspects of self? He names four: the physical, sexual, thinking, and feeling aspects of ourselves. To be complete, to be spiritually fulfilled, we need to develop all four of these parts of ourselves.

That development is hard. That development takes work and risk. And the work we choose to do to make that growth happen is love. It is the act of loving.

Let's take an example. Let's say you grew up in a family situation where you were told that you were dumb and shouldn't expect to succeed at anything "hard." You might have made choices that steered you away from developing your thinking capabilities. The thinking aspect of yourself is probably not very well developed. Well, as an adult, you're not going to suddenly start studying quantum mechanics or relativistic physics. To develop this part of you, you will probably need some help. You will need the effort and persistence of someone who can assist or guide you in developing your thinking skills. This effort is love, and assists you in your spiritual development.

The same might be true of your sexuality. If you were influenced to avoid those aspects of your emotions and ignored the physical signals from your body, you are probably going to need some help to develop a healthy sexuality. That might come from a counselor, a doctor, or a caring intimate partner. But it is going to take some effort, and that effort is going to have to be focused on you and helping you grow. That effort is love.

Love and In-Love

One From Column A, One From Column B: Now, let's start lacing these two together. Did you notice that both falling in love and love are ways to complete yourself - to fill in the missing pieces?

Now, here you are, incomplete, as we all are. There is a driving force to change that - that's why we fall in love! That driving force comes from your unconscious – your spirit and life energy. It is a drive toward meeting your need to become a complete person.

Now, you have a choice. You can allow your unconscious to continue to try to fill in those holes by falling in-love. Or, you can try to fill them in through deliberate and purpose actions of love. Which are you going to chose? Well, love is work. That's not too enticing. Falling in love feels good. Yeah, that's for me!

The problem is that falling in love has so many problems. Just as a start, falling in love limits the people who could help you grow to those who could be sexually attractive to you. What a huge limitation! Think of all the potential that's eliminated! And the other problems are big, too. Taken together, they almost guarantee that falling in love won't provide the same opportunities for a complete – and happy – you that the hard work of loving can provide.

Falling in love, if it ends up becoming a stable relationship, can provide nurturing from your partner. But by itself, falling in love is not going to fill in those denied and undeveloped parts of yourself. Only the growth made possible by love is going to do that.

No Alternative to Love

So the reality is that, sooner or later, you are going to have to get some **real** love if you're going to grow enough as a person to be complete. That means you're likely to be unhappy until you get it. And you may fall in love again and again, each time being swept up in the euphoria and distorted thinking, believing *this time* all your needs will be filled, and still not get there. If we're lucky, a falling-in-love relationship will evolve into a loving relationship, and that will help us grow. But if you know you need the real love, why not *plan* to get it? Why not get ahead of the game and look for ways to get that effortful help in growing yourself?

The great thing about real love is that it can come from anyone: a best friend; an 89 year old philosophy professor; a therapist we pay to help us; some loud mouth on the Internet; or the author of an inspirational book; even mom or dad; and of course from ourselves! Real love is about *people*, about *minds*, about *caring*; not about sex. Real love is healthy and sustaining, so you can get it where you want, when you want, with whom you want. And you can keep your head and your emotions with you. It is truly a healthy interaction.

We all need energy and courage invested in us to help us grow. We need someone – whether it is someone else or we do it ourselves – to care enough to work to help us overcome our fears, learn the things we don't know, unlearn the wrong things we've learned (that's what I'm doing here, I hope), and step onto new ground. It takes time. And it *is* work. And it's not very likely to come from falling in love.

But it is the only way to become complete as a person, and to become truly happy. And the need to complete this task will never go away. Not as long as we live. It is, in truth, *the* challenge of being human.

What to Grow?

 Great, you're thinking, all I have do is fix up these hidden and denied parts of myself… Wait a minute?! How the heck do I know what these parts are?

This is a hard question. Obviously once you break through the denial enough to see the denied parts, they won't be denied anymore. The hidden parts you probably know, if you have the courage to look. But how?

Well, I think there may be lots of ways to get at this, but the one that I think has been most definitive for me is the pointer of tears.

Remember, our unconscious communicates with us mainly through feelings. In general, things that give you a teary, hurt feeling are things that are *about* your hidden and denied aspects. They are messages from your spirit trying to draw you focus on something. I'll give you a couple of examples.

Example 1: Performing - I used to sit in my daughter's ballet recitals with tears in my eyes. There was no great mystery about it. I *knew* that I was wishing that I could perform for an audience. I was really jealous of the opportunity my daughter had. This was an undeveloped aspect of my spirit, making its need felt through tears. Well, one of the activities I've found for myself is a performing sport. It's done before an audience, and people like to watch. I didn't know when I took it up that I was fulfilling a part of myself that had been neglected. But I was, and I know now that this is one aspect that continues to draw me. And I feel very different watching others perform now. I don't feel jealous or sad; I *relate* to what they're doing.

Example 2: Help Me! - I used to find myself welling up, almost sobbing, when an ambulance would pass with lights and siren. I would think about how ambulance crews devote themselves selflessly to helping others in desperate need. This had happened for a long time, but I never understood it. Now I do understand.

I was in an unhealthy relationship for a long time. My wife controlled me and dominated my spirit. Even as I was growing and building some new aspects of myself, she resorted to more desperate and violent verbal attacks to beat me down. So what does that have to do with an ambulance? I had isolated myself from people and from the nurturing that was around me in the world. And I *needed* the help and nurture of those people. My spirit was calling out to me, "Help me!" And I wasn't listening.

Step by Step - I know these are small things, and they're about me, not about you. But I bet you have a little store of situations, places, people, movie scenes, or whatever, that give you similar feelings. These things are pointing to the areas you need to develop: aspects of yourself about which you need to find people willing to give to you, and help you grow.

Those people are out there. They're teaching art classes, on Internet support lists, at the end of the telephone line to that relative you've stopped talking to, and a thousand other places. We each have to reach out to find them.

Section 3 – Marriage

Marriage can mean a lot of things, and when we think of marriage, we might envision all kinds of situations.

From the standpoint of making a marriage work, we need some idea what is essential to marriage. And I believe that asking what is essential to marriage is the same as asking what is *unique* to marriage.

When I advise people who are in seriously troubled marriages, I tell them that making their marriage relationship work hinges on them getting from their marriage the things that marriage, and only marriage, can provide.

Marriage exists within a society – a set of norms for behavior. Some of those norms have a lot of flex. And some have very little. And there are two norms around marriage that are quite strictly interpreted in our society and our values:

- Sexual intimacy is allowed only with our spouses

- Emotional intimacy on a daily basis is allowed only with our spouses.

Once we commit to a marriage relationship, we become entirely dependent on our spouse to meet these needs. If our spouse fails to fulfill those needs, we become trapped in a state of deprivation – a state which is at once painful, difficult, and harmful to our well being.

And while a marriage may have many other dimensions, if it fails to fulfill these two critical needs, it is not going to be a successful marriage. I don't mean that it won't go on – but I do mean that happiness and fulfillment won't be found within that marriage.

So what does all this have to do with falling in love? Or loving?

Falling-In-Love and Marriage

Well, what does all this falling-in-love business have to do with marriage? Isn't it, after all, an attraction that passes with time? So is it just a lure to bring people together and be forgotten? Or does it have more lasting role?

The answer to this comes back to the role that our unconscious minds play. Remember that sexual intimacy is one of two needs that are uniquely met through a marriage relationship. Once we marry, there is no other acceptable way to fill this need.

Sexual intimacy, of course, only works when there is sexual attraction between the spouses. So to maintain sexual intimacy, we need to maintain sexual attraction. Round and round she goes! Where does attraction originate? In the unconscious! And what are the keys to generate sexual attraction? The same characteristics that lead to falling in love.

To sustain the attraction between husband and wife, the forces that draw them together need to be maintained. Thus, both husband and wife have an obligation to maintain themselves to provide the stimulus – the pattern – that will maintain attraction in their spouse.

The man's responsibility is to maintain himself in a strong hunter role. This means maintaining his confident demeanor; independence; strength; and focus on task. Moreover, the relationship is now a reality, not a potential future state like it was when the couple first met. Now, the man needs to fulfill his role as provider and protector to the marriage and the family.

The woman's responsibility is to maintain her appearance to maintain as many of the physical characteristics that trigger attraction, and to maintain a submissive role with her husband.

Today's Challenge: Unfortunately, modern western culture has developed a pattern in marital relationships that makes this difficult to achieve. As women have achieved more independence and power in the world at large, they have assumed a much more aggressive role in the marital home. Most women are naturally more sensitive to their environment and the needs of their family than men are. They tend to be much more concerned about the state of the home and the care of children. They often want things in the home to be right. Men, in contrast, often have much lower sensitivity to their environment.

The need to have the home in good order, combined with their power and independence in general, can lead wives to effectively take over their marriages, their family, and their home. In doing so, the husband is often pushed aside and is perceived as a hindrance to achieving the household state that the wife is working for. Many husbands accept this, and in a sense disengage from the family, leaving the wife not only in charge, but carrying a disproportionate share of the burden of running the family.

Of course we could speculate about how this more prominent and powerful role in the family came about. But regardless, from the standpoint of maintaining that first key

and unique contribution of marriage –
sexual attraction and intimacy between
husband and wife – it goes too far and
places a disproportionate burden on
women. It also disrupts the dynamics which
can sustain attraction within the couple.
Women in this role are no longer
submissive to their husbands, nor are their
husbands able to continue their role as
strong, confident, and independent
providers.

When I say that a wife should be
submissive to her husband, I'm not arguing
for a return to the dark ages. Women can
continue to play an assertive role outside
the scope of the marriage relationship. But
if she wants to maintain her husband's
attraction to her as a woman, and if the
husband is to maintain his attractive
characteristics, the roles of husband and
wife need to be more balanced and stay in
harmony with the key physical
characteristics and behaviors of attraction.

Husbands need to step up and play a more
prominent role in leading the family. Every
mother seems to want her daughter to marry
a "nice" man. But nice is not attractive.
"Whatever you want, honey," is not an
effective mode for a husband. It is not
confident, strong, or independent. Neither is

slipping into overweight, checked out and parked in front of the television.

These are conscious choices, and they may actually feel like they run against the grain. They certainly will require effort for both husband and wife. But the inherent dynamics that are at work when we fall in love are still operating between the couple, in the unconscious dynamics of attraction. And keeping those dynamics energized is critical to meeting that first key need only the marriage can fill – sexual intimacy. Maintaining a strong and viable relationship means working to maintain these qualities even when it feels like an uphill battle.

What about Love and Marriage?

Now after all this, *finally* we come to the ultimate question of love and marriage. Earlier we learned that love –as opposed to being in-love –is something that we do and something that we choose to do, because it takes effort. Love is work expended to help ourselves or someone else to grow as a person.

I remember as a child being surprised when I was told that plants either grow or die. They always looked to me like they were sitting still, and that seemed like a perfectly reasonable state to me. But in reality, plants grow or die. And so it is with people also. I believe it is in our nature to continue to grow as people throughout our lives. Finding happiness requires us to continue to grow.

So how does this idea of love – the fostering of personal growth – fit into the marriage puzzle?

Growth involves risk. Taking risk means becoming vulnerable. And that is not something we want to do just anywhere, anytime, because we know that people can hurt us. Our spouse plays a key role in this by helping us feel safer during those times when we become vulnerable. Our spouse needs to be a safe harbor; a shelter for those situations where we move outside our experience and try new things.

The thing about change is that we go into situations where we don't have experience. Since we don't have a history in those situations, we have to rely on faith help us maintain a healthy perspective. Faith gives us a belief that we can succeed in a situation where we have no history of success – no track record to look back on – no experience that shows us we won't fail.

Without that experience, where does the faith come from? It comes from a different kind of experience, but one that also teaches us that we can succeed. It comes from encouragement and expressions of certainty in our ability to succeed. "I know you can do it."

In a marriage, where is this kind of opening to vulnerability and the assurance of success going to happen? They require a high level of emotional intimacy and support – something that, in our culture – happens almost exclusively within the marriage relationship.

So the safety to show vulnerability and the expressions of confident support that are needed to enable growth – these make up the key actions of loving that enable a spouse to grow as a person. And because of the emotional intimacy required, it is a role that our culture requires be filled by our spouse.

Codependence and Love

Every time you read about people who are in relationships with someone with problems, you hear about codependence. The way most people talk about it, codependence would seem to be a well defined problem – something you can put your finger on and say, "There it is." In reality it is a much more vague concept, and often isn't specific enough to lead to definitive actions that could be taken to correct it.

Basically, codependence centers around the idea of one person feeling better by being involved with someone else who has problems. One way this can manifest is by feeling like you're helping or saving the person with problems. In a sense, you become a hero because the other person just couldn't make it without you – or so you feel.

What does this have to do with love and being in love? Well, they're both situations in which we get a big part of our own well being from relating to someone else. And sometimes we can get the two mixed up.

My own experience around this was triggered by Celine Dion's song *Because You Loved Me*. If you don't know it, it can be summed up in one line: "I'm everything I am because you loved me."

There was a time some years ago when I was in love with someone who didn't love me in return, and this song really wrenched at me. I *so* much wanted her to feel that I had empowered her.

Later, as I learned more, I came to associate this feeling with codependence. That is, I thought it meant that I would only feel ok if there was someone out there who needed me for her to be ok. Well, one more problem to fix. After that, I made a real conscious effort to react to this song differently - by being aware that it was generating some feelings I thought were unhealthy. Basically, I tried to turn off those feelings.

In my book *Tears and Healing* I talk about
a spirit within each of us that empowers us,
provides our life energy, tries to guide us to
be healthy, but struggles to communicate
with our consciousness. The channel to my
spirit that I discovered first was the channel
of tears. When we experience something,
usually something good, and we well up,
this is a message from the spirit. There is
something important, probably an unmet
need, relating to that experience.

I later found another, much more
controllable path to my spirit. It is through
meditation. That is, in a safe and quite
place, basically emptying my mind of the
whirlwind of thoughts, putting a simple
image in my awareness, and just being open
to what is happening. If the image has to do
with something important, my spirit
responds with emotion. It may be a
sustaining feeling, it may be tears, or it may
be a sickening feeling in my stomach.

Another way of painting images in a
meditative way is with music. In fact, music
connects with our spirit even without
meditating, but by adding the quiet, safe
space, I think we can get a much clearer
picture of what our spirits are saying. And
music was the channel by which I gained
some better insight into what I thought was

a codependent tendency in myself. Indeed, it was a LeAnn Rimes song, *I Believe in You,* that did this trick for me. This song's message is about feelings toward someone that loves you, "Your mercy has no end; you're more than just a friend. It amazes me that you feel the way you do. I believe in you."

This song helped me sort some of this out. The spiritual issue here for me was **not** that I'm codependent and need someone to need me to be ok. The issue here is one of **being appreciated** for loving someone. I never felt that my ex-wife really received or appreciated the love I gave her. No matter what I did, it was not enough. Or when it was, the way she expressed her acceptance and appreciation was very mechanical and insincere.

I don't know about you, but I really am a very loving person. And I loved my ex – and I mean in Peck's sense of caring and working for her. For years, my love was unacknowledged - unaccepted at a level that my spirit, the true judge of right and wrong, could recognize. And when my spirit senses the imagery in these songs, of love received, accepted, appreciated, and that appreciation is expressed beautifully, it sends me a really clear message. I need that. I need someone that can accept my love and show me so.

So, something that looked on the surface like a maladjustment in what I needed from an intimate relationship turned out underneath to be a fundamental message of growth for me. I do need it, and it's a healthy thing I need.

Maybe your life experiences have never led you to be aware of codependence. If so, good for you. I hope it's something you never have to deal with. But if you have bumped into it, be aware. Falling in love is about meeting needs through another person. Codependence is about meeting needs through another person. But they're not the same thing – not at all. We all need to be loved and to give love and have it accepted. That's a healthy need, and one we should work to fill. Codependence is a different thing; something not everyone needs to be concerned with, and we need to be careful not to see codependence when we look at our emotional needs and the feelings that come from them.

In the End

Falling in love is natural process. Our mind, working on a level below our rational awareness, searches for patterns in the men or women around us that signal a good potential mate. When it finds that pattern, it can generate strong feelings of attraction to pull us into an intimate relationship. By understanding these patterns, we can better deal with how and when we fall in love. While it's not the only way, falling in love is often the catalyst to get us into long term, hopefully permanent relationships.

Love is an action; something we choose to do; that helps either us or someone we care about to grow as a person. Love is not limited to an intimate partner, but intimate partners often can love one another in ways that are important and can't be done by anyone else.

In marriage, the dynamics of attraction that are at work in falling love continue to play a role. Thus both spouses need to be aware of their responsibility to work to maintain the characteristics that sustain attraction. So, too, each spouse is uniquely able to provide the love needed to support the other's growth as a person. With the right knowledge, effort, and attention, loving and the attraction of falling in love provide the foundation for a fulfilling and lasting marriage.